JUAN
BY
JUAN

BY

JUAN RAMIREZ, JR.

Salamander Street

First published in 2023 by Salamander Street Ltd.
(info@salamanderstreet.com)

A CIP catalogue record for this book is available from the British Library.

Cover photography by: Angela Reynoso (IG: LaReynaPhotos)

ISBN: 9781914228971

10 9 8 7 6 5 4 3 2 1

Wordville

Shout out goes to the love of my life, my wife, Cristy Reynoso

My folx who've done the most, Juan and Gladys

My supportive sisters, Alice, Angela, and Sammy

Wordville, for keeping the word to always deliver words to the world,

and to the best birthplace to inspire one's brilliance...

The Bronx.

About Juan Ramirez, Jr.

Juan Ramirez, Jr. is an internationally produced and award-winning multi-hyphenated artist.

Puerto Rican and Guatemalteco, he's born-and-raised in The Boogie Down Bronx. At a young age, he first explored with screenwriting and storyboarding, then creating comics for fun, he became fascinated with words, carving them in wet cement and spraying graffiti on walls, then using charcoal on cotton rag paper. Visual language took him to Hip-Hop on street corners, which took him to poetry at open mics, where music took him to discovering playwriting in his undergrad, taking him to directing, producing, acting, and writing monologues, finally picking up filmmaking at grad school. Today, he continues to create in each of these mediums.

His art focuses on giving a voice to the voiceless, artivism (art and activism), archiving stories, making the audience work, and revealing character truths in the most beautiful ways.

As a poet, his work is a two-time entry into Arte Latino Now Exhibition, highlighting and archiving Latino art, featured artist with Art Defined's Poetic Affair, IATI's Tertulia and Nuyorican Poets Café, and published in Bronx Memoir Project: Volume V. His plays were selected and performed with Yaddo, Rattlestick Theater, Repertorio Español, Bronx Council on the Arts, Pa'lante Theater, Destinos Festival with Subtext Studio Theater Company, and others.

He's a two-time Bronx Recognizes Its Own Award winner, Dramatists Guild member, Dramatists Guild Fellow, Yaddo Fellowship, resident dramatist at Art Defined, Inc., Playwriting Lab Director at MCC, NYU adjunct and Juan Man Show, LLC monologue catalogue writer, receiving his BA from Lehman College and his MFA from NYU Tisch.

For complete biography visit: www.JuanRamirezJr.com

Contents

Poems

Monologues

Juan On Juan

If I had to tell you about myself, would you believe me?
I'm ten foot ten
Devilishly handsome even for an angel
I'm too perfect for a mirror to accurately reflect me
The only problem I have is that I have no problems

If someone told you about me, would you believe them?
They may say I'm five foot two
With the face only a mother named Rosemary who birthed
    Satan's child could love
And flawed to the point where the broken gaps in my skin let
    my deep personality shine out
You could never find me unless I stopped hiding

If you made up your mind about me, could it change?
There I go, shoved to fit into your box with a label that reads
    something illegible
Are you comfortable with who I am now?
Will you ever let me out to become something else?

Maybe it was the way I smiled or
Maybe it was the surprising knowledge I held or
Maybe it was the way I was listening to you or
Maybe it was the morning light through the slightly open
    curtain and how it touched my body reminding you of a
    spotlight revealing my role in the world where an audience
    can see how well I love myself and possibly you could see
    how well I love you?

If I told you about myself, believe me
I'm five foot six
With a face I face everyday
Every crack in my body is filled with diamond, platinum,
    gold, silver, bronze, and mud
The hair on my beard is as red as the hair on my head is black
My eyes are dark chocolate drops floating on honey
Cinnamon freckles on my coquito skin
Teeth of champagne taste
Mayan and Guatemalteco eyes above a Nuyorican mouth
I'm a chilled 40-year-old reserved bottle at a reserved ten-top
    table filled with a group of highly passionate friends talking about
    great sex
An old soul ready to live life again

Can you imagine me?
I bet I can still surprise you
When I tell you about myself, believe the truths
The lies, the rumors, the hearsay, the myth, the folklore,
    and the legend
Why be anything else?

From Day Juan

The wide eyes of my mother crossed two borders
The broken lips of my father crossed many paths

I
found out I existed
when they told me to hush

I
found out I had a voice
when I spoke up

I
found out I had strength
when they collapsed

I
found out they lied about me
and never looked back

From Day Juan

I
found out I had love
when they were scared

I
found out I was brave
when they wouldn't dare

I
found out about myself
when they left me in silence

I
found peace
among the familiar fluency of violence

I
found my today
and only visit my past

I
found who I can be
and never again asked

I
found the missing piece
and it began

I
found out what I was meant to be

From Day Juan

The wide eyes of my mother and the broken lips of my father
    lay on my face

I
am armed to travel through borders and paths
to have a leg up on legacy

From Day Juan to my last days

I
take my history with me

The moment this land documented my mother and
    recorded my father

I
notated
I
archived

    Search me and you'll find
        not only one life
        but lifetimes

Like The Sound Of Juan's Own Voice

I was the first
of my friends whose voice cracked
a cuatro with one string
in desperate need of tuning
deeper it got
so did my meaning
a soft reserve I would deliver
being told my words were sharp
candid cadence
there's a performance built in.
inflections and intensions
but your assumptions
get in the way
when Juan prefers a direct message
listen
no need to waste honey on bees
or attract flies with shit
for any compliment
I give
is meant to give wings to uplift
where's the line
of what I said
and what you heard?
not always honest
but I keep to my word

I broke my moral compass
some say I'm lost
but not all sheep want to return to the shepherd
for I traded
wandering love for wanderlust
when you talking sideways
you can't talk me down
or tell me to shut up
use your diaphragm
say it with your chest
say more
say less
whether you never heard this before
cuz of ignorance or fear
I was the first
to tell you what you needed to hear

Juan Side Of The Story

To get to Canal Street
take the 4 to the 6 train
steamed dumplings
bootleg CDs and mixtapes

immigrant Cantonese and Fuzhounese women
carrying carts with merchandise
this ain't for broken pockets
no bargains for this price

we was high school adults
looking for ways to flip our lunch money
our life wasn't our fault
and the only way out was opportunity

arcade games
and when the cops came
all the hustlers ran away
but for some reason we stayed

they would only talk to me
"hey, are you with <u>them</u>?"
talking about who I came with
"yeah, and <u>them</u> is my friends"

they asked if I was okay
I say "we fine
why don't you mind your business next time?"
and they quickly realized it was I

who was trouble
who lives a life
with no space for a narrator
because I
always tell my story from Juan side

truth is
everyone down when everything is up
until everything up comes down
and upside down we stuck

they caught us
but there was no proof
they actually caught you
and you said I was there too

had to learn that being silent
could be turned into an excuse
for someone else to speak for you
and make you into a fool

you said it was me
and they believe you
today, I saw you on the avenue
I'm sorry you're the same you

but here's what I remember most
from those days long ago
your story has changed
yet mine is the same as before

let it be known
I can forgive ya but the streets won't
take the truth with ya
to the grave you go

who am I?
who lives a life
with words I paper
because I
always tell my story from Juan side

hiding behind cigarettes
and the food I feed you
I can't love you
if you don't let me meet you

I paid for movie tickets
but we never looked at the screen
taught you how to find me
taught you how to roll weed

took you out your house
to only down the block
freedom felt good
you didn't want it to stop

walked you through dangerous neighborhoods
snuck in your parents' house
bad felt so good
doing all of what your mama warned you about

read your poetry
touched each other's hair
kiss your flaws
until you decide to no longer play fair

you said I was enough
but then why the lies?
you said you needed me back
too bad it took you so long to realize

I will always give my all
who lives a life
with love as natural as nature
because I
always tell my story from Juan side

Chip on Juan's Shoulder

I carved myself
while on the chopping block
crack hands never cracking
a cut of the best slice
I took the chip off my shoulder
and at the cash cage I cashed in

Atone for Juan's Sins

I would be lying if I told you I was sorry
Because I haven't changed

Forgive me, no one
I ain't gonna learn

How dare I sit in my power and stand my ground with purpose
Purely not to please you

I don't remember trying to hurt you
But I remember meaning what I said

I'm not looking for answers but for mistakes
Because I'm obsessed with change

Trying to recall this old engine of a brain
Even at a junkyard I'm down to scrap

Let's bring up the past
Do you have the time?

I won't go without a fight
Because then how would we know who won?

Don't you dare forget what I've done to you
It was on purpose

Maybe one day I'll think of you and feel regret
I wouldn't bother to give me so much credit

Better to be right than to be happy or happy that you're right
You know, it's better to be able to sleep at night
Don't correct me if I'm wrong
I'm not ready to heal

Let me blabber and banter and babble and
    run on and on and on
Until I can't escape myself and then
Only then
Will I be alone enough to realize how alone I am

I'm sorry.

Back to Square Juan

I'm trying to find the right metaphor
Describe to you my reinvention
To let you know I've changed
Just enough to prove I'm not set in my ways

Back to square Juan

I'm trying to find the right metaphor
A chess move like Ruy Lopez had.
I am my own my pawn
Moving square by square
To where you are
Promoted to Queen

Let's try again
Back to square Juan

I'm trying to find the right metaphor
Show how I transformed.
Now souped-up sports car
my transmission heart
transfuses power in my blood
and transcends me

I'm trying to show you the right metaphor
I am rebranded
Bottled for my target audience
So market me
I am the healthy food for thought
you crave

I'm trying to fight the right metaphor
my hands raised
ready to box yet in my corner I'm cornered
out for the count

I'm trying to think of the right metaphor
To invent a formula
Juan plus Juan equals…
it all comes back to square Juan

I'm trying to write the right metaphor
A new chapter in an old book
a wrinkled page
where the coffee-mug stain circles a paragraph that shows and not tells
exactly what's happening in my life
I've only read the book once
Instead I re-read this paragraph
again and again

Trying to find the right metaphor with as much hope as
seeking out that drop of water in an ocean
splashing into
a grain of sand on a beach
moved by
a cool breeze in the heat
pushing a speck of dust
in a cloud
landing on
a needle in a silver-colored haystack

Let's try again
If only one more time

I'm trying to find the right metaphor
Wandering lost
Tripping over words like, as, such, to be
Similar like a simile
I am new…
but still the old me…
…who can't let go

And around I go

Back to square Juan

In Juan P-I-E-C-E

I'm kicking it on the 7-train tracks
When shorty doowop looks back
She waits for me to rap but I never give her the mack
I guess those are the breaks
Another black magic woman with a small raspberry beret
Reminding me of the visit I have to make

This young kid speaks,
"Shorty's checking you out.
Ask for a date?"
I say,
"Little man, life ain't always about the conquests you make
Let me explain."
But he's in a rush
With his eyes to prize another one his age walking by.

Right on time and punching in for work
this woman comes through the traincar
shouting out about "God's forgiveness."
But only if I'm "…down for the mission…"
If she thinks I'm not worth it, as is, then I ain't got time to listen
She goes on saying I'll be a "statistic"
I tell her, "I'll always be behind bars as long as I'm lyricist."
She says, "Ridiculous!"
I say, "Excuse me, miss?
Why don't we agree to disagree at your church of commuters
who'd rather look down at their phones and computers.
So leave me to believe in my amusements for a future,
to rid of me life's worries before falling into a stupor."
Not looking to make overtime
She moves on to her next victim
and gets off the next stop
turning the platform into her podium for anyone who'll listen.

This station brings along a familiar face
Homeboy I know from back in the day
He notices me right away
"Hey"
"Hey"
As small talk is made
I daydream away
About how I should come up with a pseudonym
to write best-selling erotica
so I can make lots of bucks one day
Under a name I haven't chosen yet
As he goes on about his shitty job, slutty wife, and sloppy mistakes
He realizes he's gone on for ten minutes straight
And asks how I'm doing as of late.
"Yo, I haven't spoken to you in years
and it's clear that you forgot we barely spoke then
and so we barely will now!"
That's what I want to say
So I give him a one word answer that tells him it's hard for me
to play pretend
Then he says, "Damn, you haven't changed."

Suddenly -
"We apologize for the inconvenience."

And so there's another delay in my path
I'll be late by more than half an hour
which means I'll get there in... why bother do the math?
I people watch

This three-year-old catches a fit in his seat
He lets out outrage that moves him like a spinning top
And across from me is some emo kid
one hand on his crotch
while the other puffs out a smell I could only describe as cheap pot

Like a rock and a hard place
I am stuck between two stops.
I could lose my mind
There's a time limit to kindness
And New Yorkers don't got that kind of time

My still life
Open the doors!

At last – the train moves and we're on our way
I'm one stop away – don't stop my way

I get to my destination
Where I push through the double doors
and am led through what seems like a hundred more

Where I am facing the lovely face
of Bonnie Sade
who is in the lobby Friday
when two posse papís
(like she used to say)
I paraphrase
want more from her than oxy that day

Looking at her
something in me stirs
This kind of anger makes me see blurs
I look to the DT and say, "Yeah, it's her."
He grabs the cover and reveals her
but my eyes will forever see her.

This news I give to the streets
has to be done alone
and to not incite revenge
I have to watch my tone
I preach
P.E.A.C.E
and say amends
but they take offense
and keep spelling it
P.I.E.C.E

Soon the convo gets out of hand
and a plan of a hand-off
of a handgun
to hand someone retribution
is at hand

Maybe we'd all feel another kinda way
if shorty has family or traceable beginnings
This life is a stage
with angels
still waiting in the wings

I take to an old vice of mine
and let the thoughts of her occupy my brain
She deserves to exist one more time
before I forever forgot her name
Wait, what's her name?
I believe it's Bonnie Mae
No, Lola Bae
No, Sade Babe
It's time for me to worry about me before I'm also a lost memory

And here I go
Another day waiting on the 7-train
Trying not to take life
Or rather trying not to take life for granted again
Doing the most with what I got
and not complain
Doing nothing means something
because at least there's still enough of you to wither away.
Do you think our words truly remain?
I'm not convinced that the entirety of my body won't die without pain
My neighborhood has seen too much falling apart
That all of us
Use each other's emotional broken shards
to make it through the day
I'm visited daily by death
What of me would you like today?
Arm, leg, eye, stomach, brain, heart

I'll be happy to give you my soul if it wasn't misplaced
If you can find it
It's yours to take
Because you can't survive here on hope or rage
I better get it together
For I only have this moment before I fade
So in that case
Remember the name
Bonnie Sade.

Juan Night Stand

I want you
to see you
in my eyes
the whole time
so you know it's you I'm doing this to

Come closer
Fill the hole in my soul with your raw

This three-feet valley separating you and me
needs a bridge
built of carnal curiosity
animalistic attraction
and instinctual intention
my molecules move
shaking and stirring
for where there's steam from our smoking bodies
there's fire

Come closer
Fill the hole in my soul with electricity I can taste

Without realizing
I was too late
to realize
I moved a whole foot toward you
and you moved too
with one foot left between us
I wonder what pulls you
and at the same time
we smiled
ah, yes, that will do

Come, closer

But right before
take a quick moment to look at me
and I'll look at you
it's time to know you in parts

Come, closing in

Bound for a crash course at full speed with a full tank
I hope it's everything I want it to be
I want it to be
Painful enough
that I forget the past
or my long day in a long year of a long life
and yet
in the same instant
relieving release

Boom

There you are
Pleasure pressure, please
Squeeze life out of me
Pour me
into your secrets
Lean into me
and we fit puzzle-piece perfectly
Tell me where you want to be put
Give me what hurts
to make you feel good

Don't you let go
Hand
Neck
Back
Thigh
Bicep
In my hair
Shoulder
Back
Digging into my back
On yourself
Stomach
Grabbing onto the air
Slowly
on
me

Come

Return to your glass of wine
and my last sip of whiskey
on the nightstand we broke

Catch your breath
to be calm
to sit in satisfaction
to overthink your shame
to glisten in pride

I leave love up to the amateurs

I wonder what I will remember about tonight

Hungry?

Let's try that place on the corner

Juan More Night

Yo, they lied to you
Who told you it's easy to rest?
Time management? Ha.
They convinced you that coal pressed makes diamonds
only when stressed
but coal only manifests when
carbon elements
in plants
decay
and meet their death

Yo, they lied
They quite want you to quiet quit
maybe that's why we smoke loud
maybe that's why they say no rest for the wicked
rest in peace or in pieces
Can I have stillness in nature's existence of survival of the fittest?

Yo,
We tryna bring sense to our common-ness
in a common sense
coma, since
I sensed my coma incensed-self
sage and incense I lit

They lied
but how do I fight sleepless nights?
An insomniac
desperate for a calm react
that I don't get when
I turn off the lights
?

Can't breath from the apnea
can't move from the paralysis
to sleep
perchance
to American Dream
into an
American Nightmare
wake me up from this

Is it us versus them
or us versus the rest
?

I want to

wake – more - full

but I feel

rest – less – ness

Yo,
if sleep is the cousin of death
may Father Time adopt me tonight

Yo,
What you gonna do
for the rest of your life?

The Fire In Juan's Belly

Buildings belong to the below now
bomb shelters
can withstand radiation, smoke, disease, hate, racism, sexism
as long as I stay home

She said,
"The world is on fire anyway"
I said,
"Girl, you sound thirsty
Perhaps you should filter your pain?"

He said,
"What's the point?
The world is on fire."
I said,
"Sounds like you want all the smoke
Autotune on repeat town crier."

They said,
"Hey, ain't you hot with all this fire?"
I said,
"I became the man who's always in my element
because I'm a writer
I'm always taking in the world
and to me
everything's new
and yet
everything feels tired
but to survive this climate
I became the man who controls fires."

I write story
show desire
from buyers
suppliers
to for-hires

through the grape vine
around the block
or by wire

I smell of sulfur and ash
the man who controls fire

I put the weight to paper
and call out false histories and liars

I got your tickets to the end of the world
I made a flyer

Before I go
all I can hope for is to inspire

I fan the flames
I am the man who controls fire.

A Product of Juan's Environment

I'm a product of my environment
Where the nutrition label labels me, made of hood vitamins

16 servings per container, serve me with no chaser
My serving size gotta be a hundred calories but ya couldn't bottle me

For yo daily value
Total fat is 0 grams but P-H-A-T is 100 grams
Whether saturated or trans
I'm all that and a bag
With no air
They charge for a taste and a drag

I'm not like, any type, not heavy or lite 'cuz I can't be served
along with rice or ice

With no salty bone, I could feed the dogs for days

Girl, drive-thru and this honey glaze
Enough sugar sweets to lick teeth but never give cavities
You'll shut your eyes, how sour overpowers as a bitter kisser
    couldn't keep cool in a room-temperature room, that's hot
More protein? You like that umami, ooh mami, dig in, no ketchup

Leave me out and even if forgotten, I won't go rotten
Juan of me is a batch and I'm always from scratch

I'm a… product of my environment
A remedy cure for your ailments, realigning your alignment

If you could find dirt, feel free to wash
If you have the strength, cut, slice, dice or squash
But you can't blend me at all
I'm cooked
Roast, stew, boil, poach,
steam, grill, braise

sear, simmer, season, sauté
grease, blanch, bake
ferment, whisk, mix, fry, stir fry, deep fry
or you can eat raw

Keep yo beef, I'm vegan, gluten, organic, and toxic
I can't be swallowed whole, wipe yo mouth and get yaself a napkin
If you can't handle this diet digest shiiit, yous about to, shiiiit
Watch your manners
I'm food for thought that's good enough for yo momma and nana

In the concrete jungle they at the top of the food diamond
   Cuban Link chain
Yo, ma! You looking good and yo boy weigh look the same
They wanna eat yo food, talking about lunch meat
One bite ain't the appetite they mean when they hungry
They call them burners and outta of the frying pan and into the
      fire, yo gonna be hit with a turner
Up in yo grill when they smoke you and you spill
Serving shots, but he ain't asked for refills

"Yo, ma! You looking good and yo boy weigh look the same."

I would be lying if
I told you I wasn't made of Mayan men
Street corner fire men standing by the fire hydrant but they ain't firemen
The more the diamonds bling, you could tell that retirement
      looks violent
No enlightenment or sciences can
Inspire them to stop dying, friend

In this environment
I'm a product
I watch
Boiling in my bubble,
New York City, the melting pot

As Far As Juan Knows

I boogie down to the sound
in the Boogie Down

she holds tight to a loosie now
in her loosie gown

graffiti
scratchiti
proud

there's no gentle gentrification
I'm already uptown
to be too bothered
to move on up
and live in apartments you call the Gentry

fix my park
so I can stroll
along walking trails
by
the Whitestone Bridge
where
the land here
knows Siwanoy death

where toys left in the backyard
and dinner tables of food
have been replaced
by the Moral High Ground Way
by the Live Fast Expressway
by the Land of the Free-way
by the concrete jungle
by any means
through and throughway

home is home
where the heart is
where the mind drifts
where the indigenous lived
where everybody knows your name
but even less know what you did

where you say The Bronx
and any person is familiar with
its existence

as far as I know
is as far as I can go

as far as I know
is as far as your trust can throw

lean into
your stereotypical idea
and imagine
a Bronx man
standing
on the corner
and follow him
as he walks
on
and walks
off
that block
over
the hills
under
street signs
in
other lands
out
and about
at
the edge of every horizon
to
return

as far as I know

I have a lot further to go

A Legend In Juan's Own Mind

I watch
as Destiny
looked over
at Prophecy
who then looked over
at Luck
with awe-surprised open mouths
at my success

to me
it's no surprise
how my voice
fulfills
giving this world
what it needs
in a way it wants
how lucky for you to witness

Let Juan Go

It's okay to forget me
No, really

I know our destined meeting feels surreal
painted on canvas
swirly brush strokes
to demonstrate our movement
washed away by the artist's self-hate
and obsession with mistakes

It's okay to forget me
Really, I'm not meant to stay

If you knew me for more than a moment
You may not like me
That's a lie
You would
but I like that you'll remember me this way

It's okay to forget me
and question your reality of me at all

As you struggle to think back
my brown pigment in the figment of your imagination
pixilated thoughts
your mind squints trying to recall
you'd do better to remember
how I made you feel

It's okay to forget me
because I'm not yours

Even if I live in how you now love to kiss
first cigar
best advice
filled bucket list wish

last words
final goodbye
greatest gift

It's okay to forget me
even when I needed you most

Watching you walk out the door
left over some leftovers
I never told you the depths of my self-reproach
I never told you anything since we last spoke
about how I gave up so much
and survived telling myself that there must have been some love

It's okay to forget me
because it's so like you

After lifting you up on my shoulders
standing on my tiptoes
I jump so you can make it
and up you go
I wait for your hand's reach
Hello?
It must be so wonderful up there
because it seems easy to keep from looking below

It's okay to forget me
I've done it to myself

On not having off days
I'm on week
one hundred and eighty

Standing on line
for espresso
while online

Giving into
my past time
of deadlines

Open to fast finds
of my top five vices
stopping to smell any flower
living days at a time

I once lost my name
so I could survive
burying my all
in a hallowed mine
with no signs
to return me to me
turning off the lights
to let be what be
and late one night
a voice
echo-free
letting me know it was me
told me
that all I proved
was that no one was coming
and the next morning
realizing that nothing to lose
was what I had to lose
and I was on to something
I climbed
back to the sun's shine
asking myself who was I
eyes wide
skin dried
brain fried
again, I tried
who am I?
but it wasn't until I found you
where you reminded me of

my multi-mind

my artistic liberty lies

my right to write a wright rite design

my hopeless why

and my name

as to let Juan go
is to see what's left behind
for I may never fully know me
but I'll always know when I arrived.

MONOLOGUES

13 – 17 (Teen)

18 – 25 (Young Adult)

26 – 35 (Adult)

36 – 55 (Middle Aged)

56 – 64 (Older Adult)

65+ (Elder Adult)

Late

(13 – 17)
Erica explains why she is late to class.

ERICA:

I'm always late. No matter what I do, something, anything makes me lose track of time. I'm not making excuses. I'm only saying, Mrs. Stein, today I got up at exactly six am. That's twenty minutes before I'm really supposed to get up. But did I hit snooze? No. I got up out of bed, brushed my teeth and took a shower. I know what you're going to say and, no, I was only in there for five minutes. Of course, I used soap. I'm not dirty. I even picked out my outfit in less than a minute. My hair took another minute and I still had fifteen minutes before I had to leave for the bus. So I made myself breakfast. One egg, toast and O.J.

It was the first time I walked to the bus stop. You know, because I usually have to run and Mike doesn't wait for anyone. After the first stop, the bus breaks down. Do you believe that? Everyone had to get off and the other bus didn't get there for another half hour. Then, halfway here, that bus broke down! Could you believe my luck?

So again, we all got off but this time I hailed down a cab. The driver is this sweet old guy from Poland who kept telling me how important school was. We are five blocks away when, go ahead, guess. Nope. He gets a flat tire! There was a metal fork in the road. Who eats on the street?! So I get out the cab and run over here.

That's what happened. It's the truth. Wait, where is everybody? Why isn't anyone here yet? What time is it? Please tell me it's daylight savings time. Today is the day you tutor?

Wait…did you say that it's Saturday? (*sighs*)

My Eyes Are Up Here

(18 – 25)

Marleny explains to rude men that all women know when they stare.

MARLENY:

You, aggressive-staring men, if you don't think we know that you're looking at us, guess what…? We know. Whether from far, close, talking to us, about us, we know. We see you from our peripherals. The heat from your eyes burns our faces. It's how we get acne. And we don't look because we don't want to! Hello! It's not that complicated. We are actually going out of our way to ignore you. Surprise. Although, if you had any common sense, that shouldn't be a huge reveal to you. But what do you do anyway? You stare more. You lean over and eye-linger and wait and wait - with big eyes - and wait. Do me a favor, would you? Try hard to remember that face you make when you look and when you get home, look at yourself in the mirror. You don't look how you think you do. It's getting to a scary point where women don't know whether to look back or not because on one hand, we don't want you to think we've invited your attention and on the other, we need to see where you are for our safety and, in the slight case if we're left alive to identify you. Look once. If we see you, we'll see you back. If not, better luck next time! My great body has no problem being appreciated but you cannot stay here. You got to keep it moving and let a fantasy keep you warm for the night. They call me 'Marleny with Plenty' and my eyes are up here.

For You

(18 – 25)

Danielle finally gets the courage to declare her love to her friend, karaoke-style.

DANIELLE:

Sorry, I'm sorry - sorry to interrupt! I'm Danielle. I'm here with Michelle. Well, not 'with' but we came together. I know you're next! Hold on! I'm trying to do something fucking romantic!

Sorry, again. I think everyone who has gone up to sing has been incredible. No, really. Anyway, to why I've decided to interrupt karaoke...

Michelle and I have been friends for four years. We met in graduate school and happened to live close to each other. We both also love Fleetwood Mac. Who doesn't, right? Whatever. I have been there through three tough break ups and about countless flings, I'm not saying she's a slut or anything. That's far from the truth. In fact, she waits until she truly connects to a person before even spending more time with them. Back to my point, I have always been there. And, as I'm sure you can gather for yourself by now, I'm in love with her. And, if you see the look on her face, this is news to her too. I've always found her attractive, funny and great, so this isn't something I've kept secret all this time. It happened suddenly. Okay, for a year now but that's still recent to me.

I'm a bit of a mess. Surprise! And so I never thought I was worthy of her. But that's when I noticed that all of you bitches take her for granted. I'm almost done.

No, I'm not her type, I'm not remotely good for her and I know she could do better. But she's over there – yeah, the cute one right there – she's over there telling me that after her kindness has been taken for granted, that she's ready to give up on love.

I can't let you do that, Michelle. You're too great.

Now, if you all can help me, I want us all to sing a song to her. It's her favorite song. You'll know it when it comes on.

This is for you, Michelle.

Big Purse

(26 – 35)

Maggie explains why she needs everything that's in her purse.

MAGGIE:

You don't understand! I need everything that's in here! Yes, yes, I do! Do you think I walk around with this because I like it?! It's life or death out there!

I'll prove it to you.

(*reveals or points out*) I have my wallet, my cell phone, my little bag of change because I had to separate it from my wallet because the coins kept falling out but I like this particular wallet because it has easy access sleeves for my credit card and transportation cards because I can't be digging in my purse while standing at the entry way and get mugged. Then I have a water bottle and two snacks. Each are important. For sugar intake to remain alert and the other is for energy. It's also to give to a homeless person if they ask.

Then I have two tea bags, a Vicks VapoRub, two tissue packs and a bag of cough drops. I'm always sick.

This is the self-defense book that's taking me years to read. Now, look at this.

(*shows whistle*) That's to call for help. Now this…

(*shows another cell phone*) is my back up phone to call 911 in case my first one is taken from me.

(*reveals pen*) This is my pen. It's also a pepper spray. I'm sure I don't have to explain that.

(*reveals weapon*) I haven't used this… yet.

Here are my headphones that I only keep in one ear and some extra underwear because no matter how prepared – if it happens, I may need to clean myself up. And finally, at the bottom, as always, my keys. I hold them in between my fingers like brass knuckles.

I need everything that's in here. Because for me, everywhere I go, is life or death.

Cut It

(26 – 35)

Naomi wants to cut her hair but seeks some confidence and support.

NAOMI:

I'm going to cut my hair tomorrow. Yup. All of it. I'm not going bald. It will be short. Since I was eighteen, so ten years. I don't know. Well, maybe I do. I start my new job on Monday. I started dating this woman I met at the gym. I started going to the gym. It's kind of like I'm beginning a new chapter in my life. Don't get me wrong, I love my hair. It's that representation of the strength of Solomon and all that. Although... something about me is... I don't know, maybe... it's like... I want to try... it's like when, no... okay, you know when...

I was taking my sister's terrier to get groomed. I volunteered. She's busy. The poor guy had hair covering his eyes. I watched him get trimmed and when it was done, he was energetic, wagging his tail, his entire demeanor changed.

I'm going to donate it. I'm sure I'll grow it again. People are going to be so shocked. Someone won't recognize me. Some will love it, some will pretend to love it. It'll grow back.

I don't want to be the same old me. No surprise. No mistakes. No fear. No fun.

I'm going to get my haircut tomorrow. 10am. Come with me. Please.

Involved

(36 – 55)

Didi confronts a mother about the bad actions of her son.

DIDI:

Hello, we don't know each other yet, but I'm Didi Walters. Rina's mother. She's dating your youngest son, Andie. They've been together for about two months. I believe, well, I'm sure. He's been over at my house many times. Mind if I come in?

(*denied entry*)

Okay, you don't have to let me in but you should know, Rina was crying and showed me some social media pictures your son sent. You should look at them. They are graphic. (*shows*) Maybe that one isn't of him but you can't deny the second. (*shows*) And third. (*shows*) I'm not exposing him. He's exposing himself. But I'm not here for that. I'm here because she told him to stop and he didn't. He's telling his friends she doesn't want to be a real girlfriend because she won't do certain things.

Yes, I'm always involved in my children's lives. I'm their mother. Aren't you? And if not, what's your definition of mother? If someone was sending your son - "They're not." How simple of an answer. If it's not happening to me then why care, right? You're allowing your son to grow up to treat women poorly – "I don't care." – again, great response.

I can tell you're full of hate for everything and you're raising your children to be angry like you, rather than loving, like what you could be. But that's difficult, right? That's too overbearing... to love. To treat people like people. But hey, do what you want, raise them how you want, but you better always end up on top because they'll be on the receiving end one day and you'll wish you showed that boy some guidance. He's going to need it when it really hurts. And I can't wait for my Rina to run into him, years from now, and wonder why she ever bothered. Kind of like how I'm feeling now.

I'm here because I care. Your poor son.

Be sure you and him stay away from Rina.

Rain Check Argument

(56 – 64)

Both busy, Eleanor and her husband schedule a time and day for their arguments.

ELEANOR:

Babe, I'm tired. Let's schedule this argument for another day. How's tomorrow morning sound? Fine. Then how about in the afternoon? Oh, wait, I can't. That's no good. What about tomorrow night? What are you doing? I thought you said you wasn't going to go? Fine. Whatever. We'll do it when you get back. I don't care if you might be tired. No one told you you had to go.

No, wait, we can't talk tomorrow night, I have a deadline. And I have an evening meeting with the board. I did tell you and I'm not in charge of scheduling the meetings!

You know what, let's wait until the day after tomorrow. I know it's a long time from now but what do you want me to do? And believe me, it's not a problem, because I could be mad at you for a long time and I'll remember everything I want to say. So, see you at the rain check argument.
Rain, sleet or shine, hail, thunder, lightning, acts of God – everything! Goodnight.

(*sighs*) We need a vacation. You think of a place and I'll think of a place and we'll also chat about that the day after tomorrow. Love you. Nite.

Dinner Party Story
(65+)

Regina tells the story of how she discovered her husband's infidelity.

REGINA:

I'm at a dinner party for my best friend who's celebrating the release of her first novel. She has been writing this thing since graduate school, which I'm sure you could imagine was a long time ago. There were a lot people I didn't know and I got to meet my husband's co-workers. There was his boss, Matthew - a know-it-all who actually knows it all. His secretary, Christa - the first cat lady I've ever met. And his officemate Joe. I've spoken to Joe a few times over the phone as he would be the one who picked up when Richard wasn't at his desk.

So, the time came and she read a few words from her book. We drank too much wine and we were all having a good time. Somehow, I got myself cornered in the kitchen with Joe's wife, Beverly. She talks with this voice that only dogs could hear. She said, "I have to say I really admire your strength." "Oh, why's that?" She said, "Because of how in love you and Richard are." I said, "It takes work." "It must," she said. "Especially after what he and Christa were doing behind your back."

She continued to – what she thought – was remind me of how they were seeing each other from 1998 to 2001. On and off, apparently. When the party was over, we went home and in the car I didn't talk. He didn't notice. Then suddenly, his cell phone started ringing. He picked up and said, "Hey, Joe. What's up?" Richard listened to Joe talk for about three minutes. After he hung up, it took him about another mile to gather his thoughts and finally he pulled over to the side of the road.

He confessed or actually – I rather say – told me. He was already caught. What was he going to do? He went on ranting and I stopped listening. I didn't care. Some things aren't the same when you're my age. Now I'm not saying it didn't hurt and I'm not saying that I'm too old to do anything but I haven't loved him in a long time.

It's like I've gotten my fill of love. I don't need it. I also don't know what that means. That's what scares me. I won't let his problems be mine. Now that I'm too old for. I'm going on a dinner date next week. I told him I'm visiting my folx.

Mediocrity Is Underrated

(13 – 17)

Doing bad in school, Omar attempts to justify the reason.

OMAR:

You heard me! Mediocrity is underrated. Why do I have to accomplish things? Why do I have to work so hard? Why do I have to strive to be the best? Why can't I be… as is?

I don't have to climb Everest. I want to plateau. Have you ever seen a plateau in person? The Tibetan, the Massif, Columbia – they're all beautiful. And what if this is who I am… or meant to be? I'm okay with it and you should be too.

Mom, dad, the good news here is that you won't ever have to pay for medical school or law school because I won't be anything like you. And I promise you'll never have to bail me out of jail.

Okay, okay, back to topic. So, I got a D+, who cares? Oh. I – I do care but I'll have you know that Mr. Ramirez graded the entire class on a curve. That's not good but you should also know that, although I'm not in the top half of the class, I'm not in the bottom half either. I am right in the middle! I am true mediocrity!

You see? Nothing will ever happen to me! Good, bad, nothing! No dreams of mine can be broken and no expectation will crush me under its pressure! Isn't that great?!

Okay. I'll go to my room.

Picking Your Nose

(18 – 25)

Drew explains the great pleasures of picking your nose and whoever says otherwise is a liar.

DREW:

Whoever says they are too elegant or proper to pick their nose has no idea what they're talking about! It's one of the few joys we have as a species with opposable thumbs and fingers.

Okay, you know what it's like when your nose gets heavy, there's this itch, something feels out of place and so you do the first poke to investigate. And there it is, you feel it. So, you get in there and you feel it's a good one. This one solid piece. First, you do 'the pointer'. That's the extended index and you turn it all way to get it loose. If that don't work, then you got to use the thumb. That's because you need more surface area. You're hoping it's a little sticky so it catches and comes right out. But if that doesn't work, it becomes a mission.

You use 'the claw'. It does exactly what you think. The index with a hook at the end. But then, damn. No luck. Now, you're desperate. Long fingernails. A napkin. A pencil. A wine opener. But nothing. I mean, what's the point of having long nose hairs if they don't help in a time like this? But you keep trying.

Finally, you feel it break from your nostril wall. It's getting loose. Almost… almost… almost… wait, it went back… almost – got it! Success.

I feel great and this looks beautiful. There it is. A piece of me. My ugly on display. Hello, you. And now, goodbye. It was a pleasure.

(*pretends to eat*) I'm kidding!

(*flicks at audience*) Oops. You got something in your cup. I'm a go.

Picking Your Privilege

(26 – 35)

Chad is aware of his privilege and wishes he could help more people.

CHAD:

What am I to do? I can't help.

It's not my fault my name is Chad. I didn't choose to have white parents, one named Megan and the other named Brad. I didn't decide they would own a company, send me to great schools, help me get my first internship, first job and pay for my wedding with Kelly.

I get it. I do. This country is built for me. I walk in anywhere and I'm served the best and never assumed the worst. Although, what if I told you that that isn't always the case?

They think I'm conservative.

That I only have friends who look like me.

That I don't care because I don't have to.

It's half true. I am conservative and I do mostly have friends who look like me but I do care!

The pressure from peers to look the other way, to stay in line, to keep your mouth shut, "Enjoy what you have, Chad, because it's all we got" and the idea that I have no excuse to F up… it's heavy. Because I am human. I do F up.

What if I could redefine privilege as a good thing…? Show people I want to help and call out the elitist system…? …and when someone needs help, I can reach out, grab them, and pull them up out of their pain and into a future of hope…? What if…?

I don't know if I'm strong enough.

It's all too much.

It's not my fault.

I'm only trying to survive.

I'll help. One day.

Yeah. One day.

Existential Pigeon

(18 – 25)

Ezekiel watches a pigeon he believes is contemplating life, like him.

EZEKIEL:

This morning, I saw this pigeon standing in the rain. Not flying, walking, nothing. Getting wet. Looking around. Obviously in deep thought. You could see the others taking cover under the trees, the overpath, building ledges, store awnings. But this one pigeon stood there.

What was it thinking about? Maybe he's dreading going to a job he hates. Maybe she's worried about this month's nest rent? Maybe they just not in the mood for this shit? It's got to know it exists. It wants a nice home, loving family, a reason to go through the hardships of life. Maybe there aren't any anymore.

Each rain drop feels heavy and it's exactly how it wants to be, sunk low into the earth, hidden and forgotten, hoping to spill and drain away into a hole.

Maybe it's taking a fucking shower. It was out all night, getting filled up on bird seed and its feathers are dirty so it's taking a shower. Why go to a puddle when the puddle could come to you, right?

Finally, it flew away. Off to work. To pay the nest rent. Looking for breakfast. That's when I got up out of my bed.

Real Estate

(26 – 35)

Upset and bitter over an affair, Devin fails to sell a house.

DEVIN:

Hey. Welcome. I'm glad you were able to make it. In case you forgot, I'm Devin. Yes. I was the one you spoke with on the phone. You can leave the door open. I have to change the locks to justify the restraining order.

Now as you see, we have this beautiful entryway that leads to the larger foyer. The floors are tile, so you'll have no problem sneaking in anyone if you're having an affair. This is the common area. These big windows let in a lot of light and, if you need privacy – whether that means arguments or throwing things at each other – these blinds are great!

Let's walk over to the kitchen. Isn't it gorgeous? It was my favorite part of the apartment until I caught the both of them screwing on the counter. Right there. My marble counter. I can't unsee it. Moving on.

Let's make our way to the bathroom. Look at the size of that shower. Ask my ex, you can fit three other people in there, easy!

And finally, we are at the bedroom. Believe it or not, this is where the least amount of action occurred. I can say though, it's spacious enough that you don't even have to get anywhere close to your spouse. It's like they're in a whole other place! Even though, they are standing right there... gone.

So, yeah. Did I answer all of your questions? What do we think?

Me? I'm fine. Why you ask? I appreciate your concern but don't feel bad for me. I know trash when I see it and I always take it out on time. You know, can I ask you a question? If you don't mind me getting too personal. Great. How's your credit score? And annual salaries? Well, I'm asking now because there's no point in applying if you don't have what it takes. Because...

(*emotional*) because we want people who are serious... and if you two are not serious about this... then... then don't waste each other's time. That's all I'm saying. I'm fine.

(*composes self*) Are you two serious? Glad to hear it.

Oh, let's check out the basement! There's a wonderful little closet area where the owner before us actually kept all of his skeletons. Crazy, right? Let's go!

Hit Back

(36 – 55)

Fred tells his young daughter to hit back.

FRED:

Listen to me, you have to trust me on this, okay? If anyone hits you, anywhere, at any time, for any reason, you hit them back. No, listen, I don't care what Mommy says or your teacher, they don't know sh – anything, they're afraid, but you can't be.

People are cowards. I don't know why but they are and when they want something from you, whether it's to take what you have or make you a joke to look cool in front of their equally stupid friends, they will be unfair.

They will ambush you, lie, cheat, sucker punch, spread rumors, anything to put you down because they hate themselves and it makes them feel good in the cheapest way.

Yes, you will get hit back. Sometimes you'll lose. Sometimes you'll win. Most times it will hurt. You can't be scared of getting hit because then you'll only get more hurt.

I know it's all confusing but there are no heroes. Only you can save yourself. And if it all seems like too much, then you run. Got it? I didn't mean to make you cry.

You want to know something? I was bullied. Yup. Got into a lot of fights. And met your beautiful and smart Mommy and we did the most amazing thing, created you. It's pretty cool actually. I love everything about you. But you want to know something else? Love is strong. It could be soft, warm and fuzzy but it's also strong. It's brave. Love loves itself so much, it won't let anyone, or anything hurt it. Makes sense?

Now, Daddy is going to show you how to throw a punch. Come here.

Legacy

(56 – 64)

Barry explains to his son that passing down something meaningful isn't always in the form of possessions.

BARRY:

I overheard what you said to – I wasn't – I didn't mean to hear the conversation you and your wife – Helen – were having. I happen to be – anyway. I was afraid when I had you and because I couldn't get myself straight, I was always afraid.

A father leaves his children things. Things they can use like tools, a car, antiques. Things they can use as a foundation like education, a skill set, manners. Things they'll pass down like independence, hard work, humor.

My father left me a dozen sleeves of hats. Fishing hats, sports hats, beer hats, country hats, state hats, city hats, army hats, brand-name hats, political hats, holiday hats, a hat that's two hats and a hat that says, "This is not a hat."

I refuse to stand here and rant about how I gave you food and a roof over your head. Facts are facts. I didn't do enough. Son, let me finish.

I'm not looking to blame the job market or my long string of bad luck. I want you to know I love you and you will have more to give your children than me but, if not, if this world does get even worse, it's okay. All I have is this grand piano. And let's face it, you don't play and it's better if you sell it.

I finally sold your grandfather's hats. And every penny is yours. Or rather, my grandkid's, your child. It's not much. But you should be used to that. But even though it's not much for you, it's more than you and I ever had at that age.

I did keep one hat. Which one you think?

Have That For Her

(65+)

Arnold tells the doctor to take good care of his wife.

ARNOLD:

Listen, Doctor, I need to speak to you a minute. That woman you're going to perform surgery on – hold on now – let me get this out. That woman is my wife of thirty plus years. Thirty-two, thirty-five, only she knows.

I'm sure you get a lot of people who are always telling you to do your best and you might say it's better to be objective but I need you to be completely biased on this.

I served our country some time ago, so when facing something scary, the training kicks in as it's supposed to but it's my desire to survive that keeps me going and looking forward to life. I need you to have that for her. She doesn't have a lot left for herself and I'm giving all I got.

She's a mother of three with three grandkids. She's smart, really smart, like she was top ten percent in her schooling. She's the kind of funny that's unintentional. She thinks romantic movies don't have enough tear-jerking moments. She knows how to make a mean roast. And I mean, mean. A roast with a bad attitude. And, no matter how stupid I may behave, she makes an excuse for me. And, no matter how much I fail her, she forgives me. Now is not the time to be forgiven.

So, while you're repairing her heart, know it's a sensitive one and there are people who depend on its beat. Do whatever it takes. Because I need one more moment with her. Another vacation. Another drive. Another dinner. Another conversation. For one more time, she must hear when I tell her that I love her. Will you treat her like your own?

Thank you, Doctor. I'll be right here waiting.

* 9 7 8 1 9 1 4 2 2 8 9 7 1 *